HEROES OF AMERICAN HISTORY

GEORGE WASHINGTON CARVER

Sara Cucini

LIGHTBOX
openlightbox.com

LIGHTBOX

Go to
www.openlightbox.com
and enter this book's
unique code.

ACCESS CODE

LBXZ9242

Lightbox is an all-inclusive digital solution for the teaching and learning of curriculum topics in an original, groundbreaking way.

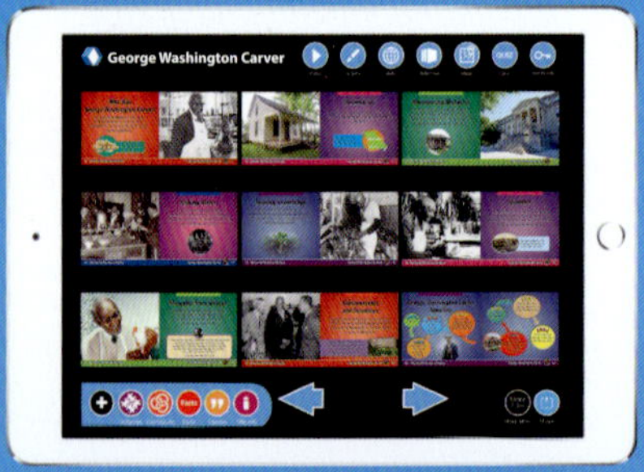

OPTIMIZED FOR

- ✓ TABLETS
- ✓ SMART BOARDS
- ✓ COMPUTERS
- ✓ AND MUCH MORE!

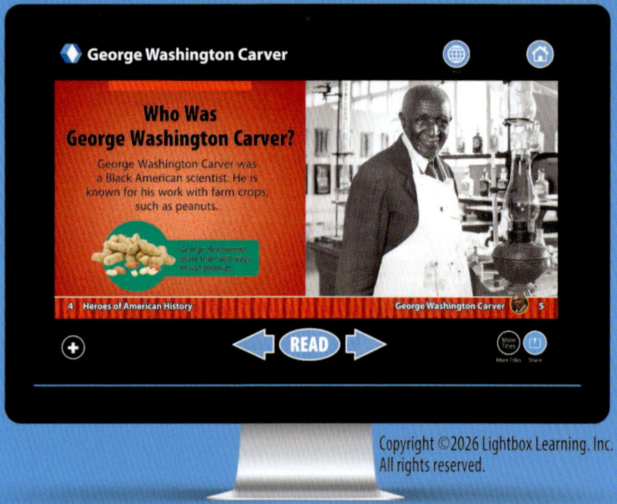

STANDARD FEATURES OF LIGHTBOX

- **AUDIO** High-quality narration using text-to-speech system
- **VIDEOS** Embedded high-definition video clips
- **ACTIVITIES** Printable PDFs that can be emailed and graded
- **WEBLINKS** Curated links to external, child-safe resources
- **SLIDESHOWS** Pictorial overviews of key concepts
- **INTERACTIVE MAPS** Interactive maps and aerial satellite imagery
- **QUIZZES** Ten multiple choice questions that are automatically graded and emailed for teacher assessment
- **KEY WORDS** Matching key concepts to their definitions

SUPPLEMENTARY RESOURCES

- **SHARE** Share titles within your Learning Management System (LMS) or Library Circulation System
- **CURRICULUM** Find national and state curriculum correlations
- **CITATION** Create bibliographical references following APA, CMSO, and MLA styles

VIDEOS

WEBLINKS

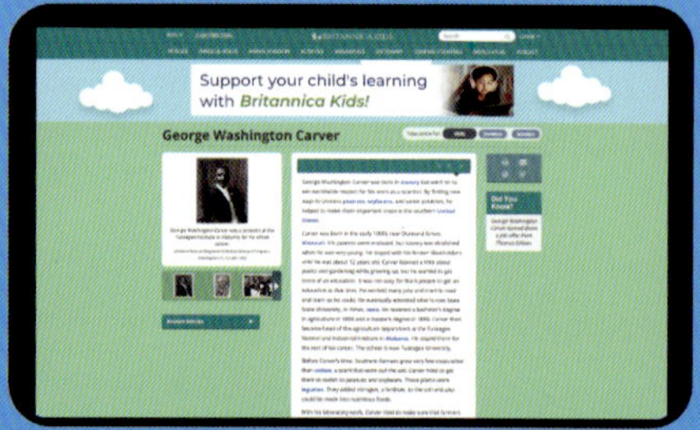

SLIDESHOWS

QUIZZES

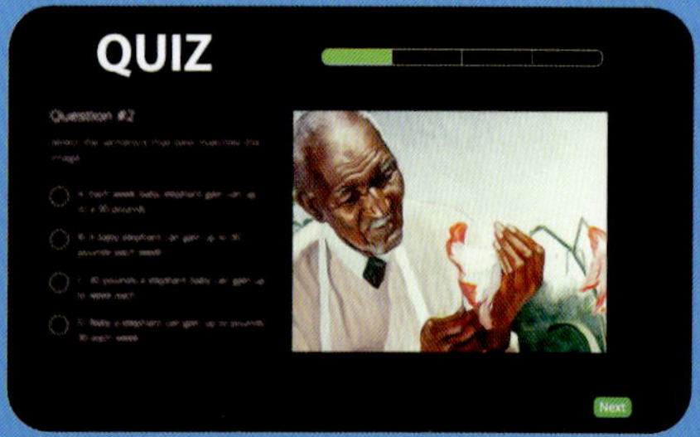

This title is part of our Lightbox digital subscription

1-Year Texas Subscription
978-1-5105-8659-8

Access hundreds of Lightbox titles with our digital subscription.
Sign up for a **FREE** subscription trial at **www.openlightbox.com/trial**

The digital components of this book are guaranteed to stay active for at least five years from the date of publication.

HEROES OF AMERICAN HISTORY

GEORGE WASHINGTON CARVER

CONTENTS

Who Was George Washington Carver?

George Washington Carver was a Black American scientist. He is known for his work with farm crops, such as peanuts.

George discovered more than 300 ways to use peanuts.

Growing Up

George was born into slavery in the early 1860s. He was freed when slavery ended in 1865.

George was born near a town called Diamond, in Missouri.

Overcoming Obstacles

In 1885, George traveled to Kansas to go to college. He was turned away because he was Black. George went to study at a college in Iowa instead.

Helping Others

After George finished college, he became a teacher at the Tuskegee Institute, in Alabama. The teachers there were all Black Americans.

Sharing Knowledge

George was both a teacher and a scientist. He worked to help farmers. He taught them how to grow better and stronger plants.

Scientist

George had a farm at the Tuskegee Institute. He used it to experiment with plants. Along with peanuts, he studied soybeans and sweet potatoes.

George worked at the Tuskegee Institute for more than 40 years.

Thoughts from George

George believed in helping others. He shared his knowledge freely. George also spoke about the importance of kindness.

"How far you go in life depends on your being tender with the young, compassionate with the aged, sympathetic with the striving, and tolerant of the weak and strong. Because someday in your life you will have been all of these."

– George Washington Carver

Achievements and Successes

George received many honors during his life. He was offered important jobs in several different places. George chose to stay in Alabama.

The George Washington Carver National Monument, in Diamond, honors George and his achievements.

George Washington Carver Timeline

1860s
Born

1896
Graduates from Iowa State Agricultural College

1896
Begins working at the Tuskegee Institute

1923
Receives the Spingarn Medal for Distinguished Service to Science

1941
The George Washington Carver Museum opens at the Tuskegee Institute

1943
Dies on January 5

1943
Donates his life savings to create a research institution

2024
Coin featuring George is released by the U.S. Mint

Cause and Effect

Cause

George taught farmers how to improve their crops.

Effect

Farmers started growing better and stronger crops.

Cause

George studied peanuts and their uses.

Effect

He discovered that peanuts could be used to make soap, ink, and gasoline.

SIGHT WORDS

Research has shown that as much as 65 percent of all written material published in English is made up of 300 words. These 300 words cannot be taught using pictures or learned by sounding them out. They must be recognized by sight. This book contains 67 common sight words to help young readers improve their reading fluency and comprehension. This book also teaches young readers several important content words, such as proper nouns. These words are paired with pictures to aid in learning and improve understanding.

Page	Sight Words First Appearance
4	a, American, as, farm, for, he, his, is, more, such, than, to, use, was, ways, who, with, work
7	in, into, near, the, up, when
8	at, away, because, go, study, turned, went
11	after, all, others, there, were
12	and, both, grow, help, how, plants, them
15	along, had, it, years
17	about, also, been, being, far, from, have, life, of, on, these, thoughts, will, you, young, your
19	different, important, many, places

Page	Content Words First Appearance
4	crops, George Washington Carver, peanuts, scientist
7	Diamond, Missouri, slavery, town
8	college, Iowa, Kansas, obstacles
11	Alabama, teacher, Tuskegee Institute
12	farmers, knowledge
15	soybeans, sweet potatoes
17	importance, kindness
19	achievements, George Washington Carver National Monument, honors, jobs, successes

Published by Lightbox Learning Inc.
276 5th Avenue, Suite 704 #917
New York, NY 10001
Website: www.openlightbox.com

Library of Congress Control Number: 2025937902

ISBN 978-1-5105-8249-1 (hardcover)
ISBN 978-1-5105-8250-7 (static multi-user eBook)
ISBN 978-1-5105-8252-1 (interactive multi-user eBook)

Printed in Guangzhou, China
1 2 3 4 5 6 7 8 9 0 29 28 27 26 25

052025
110824

Project Coordinator: Heather Kissock
Designer: Terry Paulhus
Layout: Jean Faye Rodriguez